HURON COUNTY LIBRARY

W9-CHI-275

3 6492 00427009 3

DISCARD

JUN 2 5 2001

Louis St. Laurent

J.W. Pickersgill

Fitzhenry & Whiteside Limited

Contents

THE CANADIANS
A Continuing Series

Louis St. Laurent

Author: J.W. Pickersgill
Design: Kerry Designs
Cover Illustration: John Mardon

Fitzhenry & Whiteside acknowledges with thanks the support of the Government of Canada through its Book Publishing Industry Development Program.

Canadian Cataloguing in Publication Data
Pickersgill, J. W., 1905-
Louis St. Laurent
(The Canadians) Rev. ed.
Includes bibliographical references and index.
ISBN 1-55041-495-X

1. St. Laurent, Louis S. (Louis Stephen), 1882-1973. 2. Prime ministers – Canada – Biography. 3. Canada – Politics and government – 1935-1957.* I. Title. II Series.

FC611.S24P52 2000   971.063'3'092   C00-930541-6
F1034.3.S24P52 2000

No part of this publication may be reproduced in any form, by any means, without permission in writing from the publisher.
Revised Edition
Printed and bound in Canada.
ISBN 1-55041-495-X

© 2001 Fitzhenry & Whiteside Limited
195 Allstate Parkway, Markham, Ontario L3R 4T8

Prologue

O n November 26, 1941, during the darkest days of the Second
World War, Canada's minister of justice died. Ernest Lapointe
had been French Canada's leading representative in Parliament for twenty years. He was Prime Minister Mackenzie King's closest colleague and almost a co-leader of the Liberal party. When
French Canadians heard of Lapointe's passing, they felt they had lost
a powerful spokesperson. However, they would not be without a political voice long. In Quebec City, a distinguished French Canadian
lawyer learned of Lapointe's death without realizing that it would
change his own life – and the life of the nation. For if Lapointe had
not died in the middle of the war, Louis St. Laurent would never have
become prime minister.

Mackenzie King knew he had to find a replacement for Lapointe
quickly, because a country at war cannot afford to be politically unsta-
ble. He also realized that his selection was critical: it must ensure balanced representation for both French and English Canadians.

One name that was suggested to the prime minister by several
close advisers was Louis St. Laurent, one of Canada's most outstanding French-speaking lawyers. Although he was not a member of Parliament, or even actively involved in politics, St. Laurent was known
to support the Liberal party. He also had a reputation for working
hard and being scrupulously fair-minded.

On December 4, 1941, the prime minister telephoned St. Laurent
and asked him to come to Ottawa. The lawyer was at dinner with his
wife and family when the call came and was able to guess the purpose
of the summons. His reaction was mixed: it was an honour to be asked
to join the government, but his close and happy family life was bound
to suffer if he did.

Mackenzie King scarcely knew St. Laurent, but when they met he
was so impressed, he at once offered the lawyer the post of justice minister. King suggested that St. Laurent seek election to Parliament in
the historic constituency of Quebec East, which had been previously
represented by Lapointe, and before that by Sir Wilfrid Laurier.

St. Laurent was torn. He regarded the invitation as a call to support the war, and as such, it was difficult to refuse. On the other hand,

The young advocate, St. Laurent

public life had little attraction for him and he had no desire to change his family's lifestyle. Then, on December 7, two days after his meeting with the prime minister, the Japanese attacked Pearl Harbor. Now with the United States involved, the whole world was at war. St. Laurent's mind was made up. In the face of so grave a crisis, he could not fail to answer the prime minister's call. On December 10, 1941, Louis St. Laurent was sworn into office as justice minister. He told the prime minister he was undertaking the task only as a wartime duty, and that he intended to return to his law practice as soon as the war ended.

By 1945, when the fighting finally stopped, St. Laurent had become an invaluable adviser to Mackenzie King, and the prime minister was reluctant to let him go. Knowing St. Laurent's interest in international security, he encouraged him to stay in office by giving him the external affairs portfolio. In 1947, when Mackenzie King was contemplating retirement, he persuaded St. Laurent to seek the Liberal party leadership, which he won by a large majority.

So it was that at age sixty-six, without ever having thought of pursuing a political career, Louis St. Laurent became Canada's second French Canadian prime minister.

St. Laurent had become party leader and prime minister almost by accident. The lack of long political apprenticeship did not prove a serious handicap. Less partisan than Mackenzie King, he was perceived as a national rather than a political party leader. During nearly nine years as prime minister, St. Laurent became a living symbol of Canadian unity and fostered a growing sympathy between English- and French-speaking Canadians. By reducing internal friction, he was able to secure united support for an increasingly important Canadian role in world affairs.

St. Laurent's political outlook was shaped by his family's background and his experiences as a child growing up in a rural village in the province of Quebec. As a person, he combined the cultures of both of Canada's founding peoples.

Chapter 1
The Young Lawyer

Louis Stephen St. Laurent was born in Compton, in the Eastern Townships of Quebec, on February 1, 1882. A year earlier, his father, Jean-Baptiste Moise St. Laurent, married Mary Ann Broderick, a local school teacher.

Louis was an eighth-generation Canadian on his father's side, the descendant of a colonist who came to Quebec from Burgundy in France around 1660. The family later moved up the St. Lawrence to Trois-Rivières and, in the middle of the nineteenth century, to the town of Sherbrooke, the main centre of the Eastern Townships.

Mary Ann Broderick's parents were Irish Catholics, but Mary Ann herself was raised by an aunt whose family moved to Compton from New England after the American Revolution. Though a pious Catholic, Mary Ann was imbued with a generous dose of New England puritan morality which was passed to her through her Aunt Phoebe Ford. Much of this puritan outlook would be passed on to her children and it influenced Louis St. Laurent throughout his life.

Jean Baptiste Moise St. Laurent, Louis's father

An even greater influence on the children was the fact that their father, though he could speak English, was more at home speaking French. He spoke to his children in French, as they did to him. Their mother did not speak French until she was more than eighty years old, though she could understand it thoroughly. The children always spoke to her in English. Indeed, Louis St. Laurent maintained that, until he was about six years old, he thought every child spoke one language to his or her mother and another to his or her father. Once, late in life, when Louis was asked which language he thought in, he replied that it depended on what he was thinking about and perhaps on whether he had first learned about the subject in French or in English.

The family store (and local meeting place) in Compton - Standing behind the counter are Louis St. Laurent's brother, Maurice (at right), and nephew Marc (far left).

When Moise St. Laurent moved from Sherbrooke to Compton, the village was almost entirely English-speaking and Protestant, though the migration of French Canadian farmers into the countryside was already underway. St. Laurent's general store became a meeting place for the whole community and a kind of informal club for the men. Moise himself was a regular reader of both French and English newspapers. He took a lively interest in politics and local affairs and served as an unpaid adviser to those new to the town. His guidance helped preserve harmony between the original English-speaking population and French-speaking settlers. Until he went off to college in Sherbrooke, Louis spent most of his free time in the store as an avid listener to the talk.

The St. Laurent family was very close. The children were encouraged to maintain a strong sense of duty. There was little frivolity. A

Methodist minister and his family lived next door and Louis's mother was resolved that her children would be considered as well brought-up as their neighbours. The minister's children were not allowed to dance, so there was no dancing for the St. Laurents. Later in life, Louis used this as an excuse for his inability to dance.

Louis did not begin school until he was eight years old because his mother wanted him to learn to read and write in English before enrolling in the French school. From his start in the Catholic school, Louis was always at the head of his class. The appointment of his second teacher, though, proved one of the decisive points in his life. Dorilla Têtu, a woman of great determination and intelligence, quickly recognized that Louis St. Laurent was a gifted pupil. No French Canadian from Compton had ever gone on to classical college; she resolved that he would be the first. For five years she was almost a private tutor to Louis, who quickly advanced far beyond his schoolmates. Têtu's dedication was rewarded when her pupil passed the entrance examinations to St. Charles Seminary in Sherbrooke without difficulty.

St. Laurent spent the next six years in the austere atmosphere of a classical college. St. Charles was not completely French speaking. Some of the professors were Irish priests and students were drawn from both French- and English- speaking communities. The academic atmosphere of the college was lively and St. Laurent participated fully in all activities but sports: when it came to physical exercise, he was relatively uncoordinated. St. Laurent excelled in his studies but gradually lost interest in the priesthood and decided to become a lawyer instead. He received his degree in June, 1902, with the distinction of being named best scholar of his class.

St. Laurent chose l'Université Laval in Quebec City for his law studies, rather than McGill, mainly because he did not have to pay fees at Laval on account of his strong academic record. It was a significant choice. At McGill he would almost inevitably have been absorbed into the English-

Dorilla Têtu, the teacher who quickly recognized St. Laurent's exceptional abilities

A very young future prime minister

Louis St. Laurent with his brothers and sisters.
Left to right are Maurice, Louise, Lora, Louis, Kathleen, and Nil.

speaking community. By going to Laval he was identified for life as a French Canadian.

Through the influence of the father of a college friend, John Hackett, Louis was articled to a solidly Conservative law firm of which L.P. Pelletier, a former attorney general of the province, was the leading member. Pelletier took a liking to his young clerk and was a great help in introducing him to legal practice. St. Laurent, a keen scholar, studied the law in careful detail. Later, in court, he would argue clearly and forcefully, as every effective courtroom lawyer must do. As judges noted, St. Laurent's arguments always reflected his exceptionally wide and scholarly knowledge of the law.

Unlike many lawyers, St. Laurent never considered a political career and he rarely participated in political activities, except for one brief period in 1904 when he campaigned for his father, who was the unsuccessful Liberal candidate for the provincial legislature in Compton county. Despite his association with a Conservative law firm, Louis St. Laurent always took care to identify himself as a Liberal. He was a great admirer of Sir Wilfrid Laurier, who was then prime minister of Canada. St. Laurent had no sympathy with the Quebec nationalist movement. He believed the distinct culture of French Canadians could best be preserved in a political association with other Canadians in a united country. As a young adult he never missed a chance to say so.

St. Laurent was one of twenty-five students who took the final examinations in law in 1905. The list of successful candidates appeared on June 17, with the name of Louis St. Laurent at its head. Despite his success, he was not offered a position with a law firm, so he stayed on as Pelletier's assistant at a salary of fifty dollars a month until he could find something more suitable.

In 1907, after a frustrating delay for such a promising young lawyer, he pleaded his first case. The suit, quite a controversial one, involved a priest who was charged with using undue influence to alter an elderly woman's will in favour of the church. St. Laurent's handling of the case (in which he acted against the priest) won the admiration of lawyers; but the publicity earned him a reputation, in some quarters, for being anti-clerical.

Louis St. Laurent aged twenty

A very reserved young man, St. Laurent had hitherto apparently shown little interest in women. In 1906, however, he was encouraged by his friend, Marius Barbeau, to attend a party. There he met a young woman from Beauce County named Jeanne Renault.

Barbeau and St. Laurent had been classmates and close friends at Laval. When they graduated, St. Laurent was offered one of the

Louis and his fiancée, Jeanne, in Compton in 1908

recently established Rhodes Scholarships to study at Oxford University in England. Feeling that it was time he started earning a living, St. Laurent turned the offer down, and advised Barbeau to apply in his place. Barbeau won the scholarship to Oxford and began the studies which later made him Canada's leading anthropologist.

Now, in 1906, Barbeau repaid his debt by promoting the friendship between his shy friend and the vivacious young woman from Beauce County. Though neither Louis nor Jeanne confessed it at the time, it was love at first sight for both of them. The courtship, encouraged by Barbeau, proceeded smoothly. Their families met and approved of one another. Their only objection to

The Renault's home, Beauceville, where St. Laurent's wedding was celebrated

Louis and Jeanne on their wedding day, May 19, 1908

the marriage was Louis's meagre income. When he formed a partnership with another outstanding young lawyer, Antonin Galipeau, this last obstacle was removed.

The marriage was performed at Beauceville, the bride's home, on May 19, 1908, and the young couple made the fashionable honeymoon excursion to Niagara Falls. The trip was cut short after one week when St. Laurent was summoned back to Quebec by urgent legal business.

Both law practice and family grew rapidly. By 1912 the St. Laurents had three children, Marthe, Renault and Jean-Paul. Louis had now established a practice of his own and secured his first substantial client, the pulp and paper company headed by Sir William Price. The St. Laurents were soon able to build a large, comfortable house on Grande Allée, in a new and fashionable quarter of Quebec City. This house, which they first occupied in 1913, remained their home for the rest of their lives. Two more children, Therese and Madeleine, were born there.

The outbreak of the Great War in 1914 touched the family very little. St. Laurent stated later in life that he had regarded the war as a European struggle in which Canada had no vital interest. In any event, his age (thirty-two when war broke out) and his family responsibilities would have made active participation unlikely.

The only setback to his flourishing legal career came in 1917 in the form of an illness which doctors feared might be tuberculosis. They prescribed complete rest and fresh air. Fearing a prolonged absence might destroy his law practice, St. Laurent began to talk of taking up farming. This project was ridiculed by the whole St. Laurent family at Compton, who were familiar with Louis's lack of physical aptitude. Rather sheepishly, he decided instead to spend the summer resting in the country, and by autumn he had completely recovered. He had almost no illness during the rest of his working life.

St. Laurent pleaded his first case before the Supreme Court of Canada in 1911. He was to appear there on more than sixty occasions before joining the government in 1941. During his years in practice, the Judicial Committee of the British Privy Council in London, England, was the final court of appeal for Canada. St. Laurent first went to the Privy Council in London in 1920 and returned nearly every year until he gave up practice.

Louis St. Laurent was becoming more and more a "lawyer's lawyer," frequently acting for federal and provincial governments. He was a very persuasive advocate. One of the judges before whom St. Laurent often pleaded remarked that usually, when he was hearing a case, the lawyer on one side seemed to make a slightly better presentation than the other; but after listening to a plea by St. Laurent, the judge could never see how any reasonable person could reach a different conclusion than that offered by St. Laurent. His powers of persuasion would later be very useful in Parliament and during elections.

St. Laurent worked very hard at his profession and devoted almost all his leisure to his family. He was an interested observer of public affairs but avoided party politics, to the extent that even some of his colleagues were unaware of his party allegiance. In fact, he did not waver in his support of the Liberal party, though he was never an uncritical partisan.

Graduation, 1902

St. Laurent was also one of the founding members of the Canadian Bar Association which was formed in 1914. Some French-speaking lawyers in Quebec feared that an association with lawyers from other provinces would weaken their attachment to the distinctive civil law of Quebec. St. Laurent, on the other hand, felt that acquaintance with the law and lawyers of other provinces would strengthen their appreciation of their own legal system. He also hoped the Canadian Bar Association would develop mutual understanding and foster Canadian unity.

In September, 1920, St. Laurent accepted an invitation to speak at the annual meeting of the Bar Association. His theme was the civil law of Quebec, and his speech emphasized the ways in which the two systems of law in Canada complemented each other. He included an appeal for tolerance and understanding between the two linguistic communities. This 1920 speech set out St. Laurent's concept of Canada which he was to repeat, substantially unchanged, for the rest of his life. The promotion of the kind of harmony between English- and

The Young Lawyer

Jeanne St. Laurent with her first three children, Marthe, Renault and Jean-Paul

French-speaking Canadians which existed in his own family, in the village of Compton and in the Eastern Townships of Quebec, was the cause closest to his heart.

St. Laurent became president of the Canadian Bar Association in 1930, succeeding Prime Minister R.B. Bennett. He was also elected to a second term in 1931. His prominence in the Association and his growing reputation as a lawyer made him a familiar legal figure throughout Canada.

During the 1930s, Canada was gripped by economic depression. As federal and provincial authorities argued over responsibility for relief programmes, it became clear that a drastic re-adjustment of federal-provincial financial arrangements was necessary. In 1937, the Mackenzie King government appointed a royal commission headed first by Ontario's chief justice, N.W. Rowell, and later by Joseph Sirois. The commission was created to examine relations between the provinces and the federal government. Louis St. Laurent was appointed one of its two legal advisers.

Travelling across the country with the commission, the eastern lawyer encountered, for the first time, the problems faced by western provinces; his outlook was considerably broadened. St. Laurent soon became convinced that, if national unity was to be preserved, radical steps were needed to correct financial inequalities among the provinces. Federal-provincial financial relations were to be one of the main problems he would have to deal with during his years in government.

Chapter 2
A Reluctant Minister

The outbreak of war in 1939 postponed action on the problem of federal-provincial relations, and diverted public attention to an even more controversial topic: conscription.

The introduction of compulsory military service during World War I had created a long-lasting division between English and French Canadians. When war broke out again, all political parties in Canada promised not to introduce conscription for service *outside* Canada. When France fell and Western Europe was overrun by Nazi Germany in 1940, conscription for military service *inside* Canada was introduced, but the pledge not to use conscription for overseas service was written into law. In the summer and autumn of 1941, public pressure in favour of conscription for service outside Canada began to mount. The Conservative party, under new leader Senator Arthur Meighen, changed its policy and came out in favour of total conscription, which Meighen called "national selective service."

Louis St. Laurent in 1936

When Louis St. Laurent entered government on December 10, 1941, the Liberals were already formulating their position against the Conservative campaign for overseas conscription. Prime Minister Mackenzie King was determined not to have conscription used for service overseas and he was supported, within the cabinet, by P.J.A. Cardin, the senior minister from Quebec. On the other hand, J.L. Ralston, the minister of defence, refused to rule out the possibility that conscription might become necessary. To avoid confrontation with either his cabinet colleagues or Parliament, Mackenzie King hit on the idea of holding a referendum. The voters were to be asked whether they would release the government "from any obligation arising out of any past commitment restricting the methods of raising men for military service," which amounted to asking whether they would support conscription if it appeared necessary.

Mackenzie King expected that a substantial majority would vote to release the government from its anti-conscription pledge. He explained that a release from the pledge would not necessarily mean that conscription would be introduced: it would merely leave the government free to conscript men if a pressing need arose. Both Ralston and Cardin reluctantly accepted this compromise. St. Laurent did not hesitate to support it.

By-elections had been called in Quebec East and in three other constituencies for February 9, 1942. It was assumed St. Laurent would be elected easily in Quebec. It was also expected that Meighen would be elected in the Ontario riding which had been vacated for him. The referendum on conscription was announced in the Speech from the Throne which opened Parliament on January 23. It was badly received by anti-conscriptionists. Inevitably, the conscription issue became a factor in the forthcoming by-elections.

Several Liberal organizers in Quebec East refused to back St. Laurent unless he gave an unequivocal pledge never to support conscription. He refused to give such a promise, and said the safest course for the people of Quebec was to trust the judgement of the prime minister. It was soon clear that opposition to conscription was as strong as ever in the French-speaking areas of Quebec, and the outcome of the

The war committee of the Canadian cabinet, 1943. Seated left to right: C.G. Power; T.A. Crerar; W.L. Mackenzie King; J.L. Ralston; J.L. Ilsley; standing left to right: A.L. Macdonald; J.E. Michaud; C.D. Howe; L.S. St. Laurent

by-election remained in doubt right up until election day. In the end, St. Laurent won against an extreme nationalist by a comfortable majority. To the surprise of the prime minister and most observers, Arthur Meighen was defeated by a Co-operative Commonwealth Federation (CCF) candidate in Ontario.

Louis St. Laurent became a member of Parliament nine days after his sixtieth birthday. Though he had won the by-election, it was far from clear whether he would have the support of the Liberal members of Parliament from Quebec. A dozen of them had already announced their opposition to the referendum, and relatively few of the rest were willing to campaign actively for a yes vote. The conscription referendum was held on April 27. There was an overwhelmingly negative vote in almost all Quebec constituencies except those with English-speaking majorities. There was a massive affirmative vote in most of the rest of the country.

In spite of the referendum vote, the government remained divided. Most French-speaking members maintained opposition to compulsory overseas service, while a group of Liberals headed by J. L. Ralston favoured immediate conscription. The third and largest group of Liberals in Parliament was prepared to follow the lead of the prime minister. St. Laurent was in the forefront of this group, even though it isolated him from most of the members from his own province. The prospect that he might one day be the spokesperson of French Canadian Liberals seemed very dim indeed.

Arthur Meighen resumed leadership of the Conservative party in 1941 to advocate conscription for overseas military service

St. Laurent's mother, surrounded by her children. From left to right are Louis, Maurice, Nil, Lora and Kathleen.

Mackenzie King once more tried to compromise. In Bill 80, he proposed an amendment to the law which would permit conscripts to be sent overseas, but only in cases of emergency. The slogan for the new policy (borrowed from the *Toronto Star)* was, "not necessarily conscription, but conscription if necessary." The compromise was not accepted by the whole cabinet. Cardin, the senior minister from Quebec, resigned in protest and most of the Liberal MPs from Quebec announced they would vote against the bill.

The war leaders: President Roosevelt, Prime Minister Mackenzie King and Prime Minister Churchill in Quebec, 1943

Bill 80 was passed only after two months of difficult debate, during which St. Laurent's powers of persuasion and explanation were often needed. Once the bill became law, the crisis, which had been so intense, seemed to evaporate. Meighen was no longer in Parliament to press for conscription and, more important, conscription for overseas service did not prove necessary. Voluntary recruiting was providing enough soldiers. Through the rest of 1942, the whole of 1943 and until October 1944, the divisive issue of conscription seemed to have vanished.

All the while, St. Laurent was becoming a steadily more effective member of government. In cabinet, the prime minister relied increasingly on his judgement and his loyalty. In Parliament, he was not spectacular, but usually more than competent. His debating style was like that of a lawyer in court rather than that of a politician, and he seemed ready to judge issues on their merits, not on partisan grounds. As a result, St. Laurent won the respect of the House. However, he had not

A Reluctant Minister

yet been accepted as the spokesperson for French Canada when, in the late fall of 1944, the second conscription crisis occurred.

The Canadian army had been in action since 1943, first in Italy and, after D-day, in France as well. The rapid progress of the Allied armies through France in the summer of 1944, the success of the Italian campaign, and the Soviet advances in the east left no doubt that Hitler would be defeated. It seemed highly unlikely that the use of conscripts from Canada would be necessary to win the war. It was, therefore, a tremendous shock to the prime minister when the minister of defence returned from visits to Canadian troops in Europe with a report that there would soon be a shortage of reinforcements. The number of replacement troops needed was greater than the number of volunteer recruits available. Ralston proposed to fill the gap by sending overseas a number of trained conscripts serving in Canada. Anticipating a storm of protest, the prime minister refused to accept the proposal and for nearly two weeks the cabinet wrestled with the problem. It was soon common knowledge that the government was divided over conscription. Public agitation developed on both sides.

Desperately looking for a way out of the crisis, Mackenzie King turned to General McNaughton, commander of the army from its formation until 1943 and something of a national hero. McNaughton believed he could secure enough voluntary recruits to reinforce the army, making it unnecessary to send conscripted men overseas.

McNaughton was hastily made minister of defence in Ralston's place. He took office on November 1, and at once began his drive for recruits. Those both inside and outside Parliament who favoured conscription became more and more frustrated. They felt that political procrastination was preventing Canada from doing its duty in a time of great need. Ministers threatened to resign. Parliament was summoned for November 22 to face the crisis.

On November 21, senior army staff officers called on the minister of defence and informed him that the campaign for volunteers had failed. Unless the government agreed to use conscripts to provide the desired reinforcements, the officers would resign. Reluctantly, McNaughton carried this ultimatum to the prime minister.

Faced with a possible breakdown in either the government or the armed forces or both, Mackenzie King realized that he could compromise no more. He accepted the recommendation that conscripts be sent overseas and sent for St. Laurent at once to inform him of the proposed change of policy. Throughout the crisis St. Laurent had been, at times, his sole adviser.

St. Laurent was shocked to hear that the government was apparently yielding to a military coup. Mackenzie King persuaded him that the military officers were not seeking to take over the government and

Many people were strongly opposed to sending young soldiers to fight abroad. Cabinet minister C.G. Power, who had been awarded a Military Cross for his service in World War I, was resolved in his opposition: "I went, I returned, I will not go back and I will send no one."

As the battle raged in Europe, the House battled the conscription crisis. Here an artillery tractor tows an anti-tank gun during the advance near Moro River, Italy, Dec. 1943.

that, if McNaughton's recommendation was not accepted, the government could not carry on. He convinced St. Laurent that no other viable government could be formed and that a bitterly contested wartime election would be inevitable. If that happened, the reinforcements would not be provided, the whole Canadian war effort would be discredited and the country would be divided for at least a generation. St. Laurent agreed to support the change of policy.

The prime minister realized that St. Laurent's support was crucial to the survival of the government. If St. Laurent resigned, the other ministers from Quebec would certainly leave too. If that were the case, a conscriptionist coalition without support in French Canada, similar to the Union government of 1917, would be the only alternative. Such an alternative was to be avoided. St. Laurent was able to persuade the French-speaking ministers from Quebec to remain in cabinet. The only resignation came from C.G. Power, one of the defence ministers.

St. Laurent could not be accused of a breach of faith, because he had never given any pledge not to accept conscription. He knew he was supporting a policy opposed strongly by his own constituents and the great majority of French-speaking Canadians. Such courage won him reluctant respect in Quebec and the regard of fellow members of Parliament. Before a vote of confidence in the government's handling of the conscription crisis was taken, St. Laurent provided Liberals in French Canada with a respectable defence for his government's decision to send conscripts overseas. His genuine sympathy for those Liberals who did not provide a vote of confidence in the government was what kept them in the Liberal party.

As the end of the war approached, St. Laurent prepared to leave the government and return to his home and law practice in Quebec City. He missed his family badly during the war years, living in a cheerless hotel apartment in Ottawa while his wife maintained their house on Grande Allée. Now they both looked forward to his return to private life. Mackenzie King, however, had other plans. The prime minister had already confided to his diary that St. Laurent would be his choice as leader of the Liberal party when he retired. For the time being, he contented himself with persuading St. Laurent not to step down before the 1945 election.

St. Laurent's prestige in Parliament and in the country at large was enhanced when the prime minister chose him to be deputy head of the Canadian delegation to the founding conference of the United Nations. The conference opened in San Francisco in late April, 1945. In mid-May Mackenzie King had to return home to begin the general election campaign, leaving St. Laurent head of the delegation.

The Liberal party did not have much organization in Quebec. Many of the province's Liberals had been upset by the government's policy change regarding conscription. C.G. Power, a main Liberal organizer in previous elections, said quite tongue-in-cheek that the new election catchphrase was, "not necessarily Mackenzie King, but Mackenzie King if necessary." As election day approached, however, there was an almost spontaneous rallying in Quebec to the prime minister's leadership. St. Laurent won an overwhelming majority in Quebec East, a personal triumph which surprised rank-and-file Liberals and greatly increased his prestige. The Liberal party emerged from the election with a small but clear majority in the House of Commons.

When Parliament met on September 6, 1945, the fighting was over in the Pacific as well as in Europe. St. Laurent's wish and intention was to return to his law practice as soon as he could disengage himself from government. The prime minister was no less resolved to retain the minister he considered the ablest and wisest of his colleagues.

St. Laurent was indispensable to the Liberal government for many

The St. Laurents with their daughters Left to right: Madeleine, Marthe, Louis, Jeanne, Therese

reasons, one being his experience in the August 6 post-war conference on federal-provincial relations. St. Laurent had had a large share in preparing the proposals submitted to the conference. Because of his pre-war association with the Royal Commission on Dominion Provincial Relations, he had a more thorough knowledge of the situation than any other minister. His legal and constitutional experience was invaluable.

St. Laurent was needed in the government for another reason of which the public was unaware for many months. On September 5, 1945, a clerk named Igor Gouzenko defected from the Soviet Embassy in Ottawa. He carried with him a number of secret documents which disclosed the existence of a spy ring operating in the Canadian civil service. As minister of justice, it was St. Laurent's responsibility to deal with a problem never before encountered by a Canadian public figure. The spy ring had connections with Soviet espionage in Britain and the United States. After months of investigation and consultation with the British and American governments, the alleged spies were arrested in

Ottawa on February 15, 1946. Without being charged with any offences, they were detained for questioning by a royal commission. Their detention, *incommunicado*, without disclosure of names and without access to lawyers, led to charges of civil rights violations. The opposition later discovered their detention had been authorized by a secret order-in-council signed by St. Laurent himself. St. Laurent had earlier denied there were any secret orders-in-council still in force. It was embarrassing for the government, and it was the most awkward moment of St. Laurent's political life.

The justice minister confessed frankly to Parliament that he had quite forgotten that the order was secret and based on the War Measures Act. It was a remarkable tribute to his credibility and to the respect that was felt for him in Parliament that his explanation was accepted.

That was not the end of the Gouzenko affair, however. The detention of the suspects dragged on too long amidst mounting criticism of the government and the minister of justice. In the end, many of the suspects who were brought to trial were not convicted. The handling of the spy crisis did not look very professional, but it did St. Laurent no lasting political damage.

On the contrary, when Mackenzie King went to Paris in July, 1946, to attend a conference to negotiate peace with Italy, he made St. Laurent acting prime minister in his absence. Parliament was still in session. St. Laurent led the House in a fashion so skillful and conciliatory that it won praise from both sides of the House. He emerged as the unquestioned second-in-command to the prime minister.

Chapter 3
Uncle Louis

Uncle Louis on the campaign trail

St. Laurent still planned to retire from government soon after Mackenzie King's return from Europe. The prime minister, however, sensed that St. Laurent had developed a growing interest in efforts to prevent another world war, just as Parliament changed the law so that the prime minister was no longer automatically secretary of state for external affairs. Mackenzie King hoped that by offering the external affairs portfolio to St. Laurent, the opportunity to work for peace and security might entice him to stay in government a little longer. The prime minister was most pressing in his requests that St. Laurent accept the offer. On September 3, 1946, St. Laurent gave way and agreed to become minister of external affairs, at least for the year. On the same day, Lester B. Pearson was appointed his deputy. This marked the beginning of a historic partnership in the conduct of Canada's relations with the rest of the world. It would last until June 21, 1957. Mackenzie King was delighted when St. Laurent told him, later in the month, that he was prepared to carry on through the parliamentary session of 1947.

In 1947, Mackenzie King was absent from Parliament more than once because of ill health. St. Laurent served as acting prime minister on these occasions. He carried an increasing burden of responsibility even when the tired and ailing prime minister was present. In September, 1947, the prime minister told the cabinet he would announce his retirement before the end of the year and call a Liberal party convention for August, 1948, to choose his successor.

Mackenzie King had almost given up hope of persuading St. Laurent to seek the leadership. He was therefore surprised and delighted when, in October, 1947, St. Laurent spontaneously indicated that he was willing to be a candidate. As a French Canadian and Catholic, his only fear was that his candidature might cause division within the Liberal party on cultural or religious grounds. Wilfrid Laurier had said a French Canadian would never again be prime minister of Canada. Now, as an affirmation of national unity, St. Laurent hoped to prove Laurier wrong. A relieved Mackenzie King was confident that he had found his successor as party leader and prime minister.

Louis St. Laurent with W.L.M. King at the national Liberal party leadership convention in Ottawa, 1948

Yet St. Laurent's future as leader was almost destroyed by a crisis in the cabinet which arose quite unexpectedly before the end of the year. While Mackenzie King was in London in November, 1947, for the marriage of Princess Elizabeth, Canada came under pressure from the United States to serve on a United Nations committee to supervise free elections in North and South Korea. The Canadian government agreed. But when Mackenzie King learned of the decision, he became outraged, and demanded that it be reversed. He had a premonition that another world war might break out over Korea, and he did not want Canada to get involved. St. Laurent, who had headed the government in Mackenzie King's absence, felt that a repudiation of his decision would destroy faith in his ability to govern, and make the cabinet look foolish. Usually a mild and conciliatory man, St. Laurent could nevertheless be adamant on points of principle. On this occasion he told the prime minister that if Canada withdrew from the Korean Commission, he would resign. Too valuable to be sacrificed,

St. Laurent prevailed in the battle of wills. From that time on, Mackenzie King took care to avoid clashes with the man he wanted to succeed him.

Meanwhile, at the external affairs ministry, St. Laurent and Pearson made Canada more and more active in the United Nations, and in other international concerns. Mackenzie King privately worried about this dynamic leadership until the Communist coup in Czechoslovakia in March, 1948 shocked him into recognizing the need for new international security arrangements. He agreed to join the United States in support of the newly formed Western Union of Britain, France and the Benelux countries. Western Union was the first step in the formation of the North Atlantic Alliance which St. Laurent and Pearson did much to promote.

Mackenzie King announced his decision to retire as leader of the Liberal party on January 20, 1948. St. Laurent had a series of meetings in Winnipeg right after King's announcement. In reply to an unexpected question, St. Laurent stated he was prepared to be a candidate "if it was something which would further, rather than retard, Canadian unity." He did nothing more to advance his candidacy beyond assuring himself that if he became leader, C.D. Howe would support him and serve under him in the government.

St. Laurent won the party leadership overwhelmingly on the first ballot at the convention on August 7, 1948. He did not become prime minister at once, but quickly set about organizing his cabinet. As a first step, with the prime minister's approval, he persuaded Lester Pearson to join the government as minister for external affairs.

Mackenzie King became seriously ill at a conference of Commonwealth leaders in London in October and sent for St. Laurent to replace him. On Mackenzie King's return to Ottawa, St. Laurent succeeded him as prime minister, the formal transfer of power taking place on November 15, 1948. He retained all the ministers who were then in cabinet and added the premier of Manitoba, Stuart Garson, and an able and energetic young Nova Scotian engineer, Robert Winters.

When Parliament met in January, 1949, the new prime minister faced a new leader of the Opposition. The Progressive Conservative party had held a convention in October, 1948, and had chosen the premier of Ontario, Colonel George Drew, as its leader. Drew and St. Laurent continued to face one another for the next eight years. The contrast between the two was striking. Drew's conduct was flamboyant, his language often extravagant and emotional. He had a military bearing and at times a rather arrogant manner. St. Laurent was modest in his bearing and usually moderate in language, though candid and straightforward in expressing himself. His attitude was dignified and

rather reserved, but without the slightest trace of arrogance. St. Laurent was sixty-seven on February 1, 1949; Drew was not yet fifty-five, though the difference in age was not very noticeable, as St. Laurent looked much younger than his years. St. Laurent had already been in the government for eight years and the Liberal government was aging. Drew was a new face on the federal scene, but well known from his participation in federal-provincial conferences. He had worked closely with the premier of Quebec on those occasions and counted on Duplessis to help him gain support in French Canada.

Prime Minister St. Laurent pays his final respects at the funeral of Mackenzie King, whose body lay in state in the Houses of Parliament

For the first few weeks after Parliament met in 1949, Drew appeared to have every advantage. He was widely expected to win the next general election later in the year. Within three months, St. Laurent was obviously gaining ground in Parliament. His growing strength was reinforced by two outstanding achievements. First, under his leadership, Confederation was completed when Newfoundland joined Canada on March 31, 1949. Second, St. Laurent and Pearson

Uncle Louis

had been jointly responsible for Canada's part in the formation of the North Atlantic Alliance, an organization intended to promote the common security of the United States, Canada and most of the countries of Western Europe. Both achievements met with almost universal approval in Canada.

Aware that an election must soon be held, the new prime minister set out systematically to make himself known to the public. From the beginning of 1949, he visited a different place in Ontario or Quebec every weekend. His wife and often another member of the family travelled with him. The publicity given these visits was extensive and usually favourable. On one of these excursions, during a long Easter recess, the St. Laurents and their eldest daughter travelled by train through the West to the Pacific coast and back to Ottawa. There were visits to main centres and whistle stops all along the route. Thousands of people saw the new prime minister and hundreds heard him speak. There were many children on station platforms. They gathered around him and listened attentively to his brief and simple speeches. Watching him with the children, one of the journalists dubbed him "Uncle Louis" and the nickname followed him throughout the rest of his career. St. Laurent had hitherto been respected for his dignity, integrity and fair-mindedness, but some Liberals had feared that his reserved manner might fail to win voters. Now, as he visited community after community, shaking hands, listening to problems and making impromptu speeches, St. Laurent proved beyond doubt that he was also a very charismatic politician. As his popularity

Newfoundland becomes the tenth province to join Canada on March 31, 1949.

Uncle Louis

increased, so did his confidence; with informal groups he lost his reticence and at speaking engagements he frequently abandoned his prepared notes to appeal more directly to his listeners. A well-to-do French Canadian from the East, he charmed Western Canada. The Winnipeg *Free Press* reported:

In Mr. St. Laurent the public has found at last the stuff of Canada, a French Canadian who is half Irish, speaks English with no trace of French and might have been brought up in Halifax, Winnipeg or Victoria.

The western trip was such a success that the prime minister decided to wind up the parliamentary session within a week of his return and call an election for the end of June.

The election campaign was well organized. St. Laurent rarely mentioned his opponent. He spoke in simple terms, stressing that the Liberals were the most experienced and trustworthy guardians of

Newfoundland is welcomed into Confederation, Peace tower, Ottawa, April 1, 1949. In forefront from left are Louis St. Laurent, Viscount Alexander of Tunis, Joey Smallwood, and Mackenzie King.

Canada's future. As the campaign went on, the response was more and more enthusiastic. When the votes were counted on June 27, 1949, St. Laurent had won 192 of the 262 seats and the Progressive Conservative Opposition was reduced to 41 seats. It was the greatest victory in any election up to that time.

The election of 1949 marked the high point of St. Laurent's popular support. He had revived a political party which had been in office for nearly thirteen years and brought it to the peak of its Parliamentary strength. He could not hope to increase or even maintain that strength. At the time, it seemed he would never face another election, for he would be over seventy when the next was held. But St. Laurent was, in fact, to contest two more elections and remain in office for another eight years.

On his first day as prime minister, St. Laurent stayed in his office working with one of his secretaries until nearly eight o'clock. When he left the second-floor office, the elevator operator was waiting to take

Enthusiastic St. Laurent supporters at a campaign rally during the 1949 election

him down to the ground floor. St. Laurent asked him why he had stayed so late. The man replied that he always stayed until the prime minister left the building, however late it was. "From now on," St. Laurent told him, "leave at the end of the normal working day. I can still walk down one flight of stairs!"

Such consideration was characteristic of his attitude toward his staff. Indeed, his style of working was in marked contrast to Mackenzie King's. His predecessor usually worked in his library at Laurier House unless specific business required his presence in Parliament or the cabinet. He was nearly always late for appointments and meetings, and there was no system or order in the way he dealt with official papers. He did not like to be disturbed even by his ministers, and it was often difficult to get him to see even important visitors such as provincial premiers. But when he decided that something should be done, it had to be done immediately.

St. Laurent, on the other hand, kept regular hours, worked every morning in his office, and disposed of official business promptly and in an orderly fashion. He was always readily accessible, especially to his ministers, and never interfered with their departments without consulting them first. He tried to clear all official papers off his desk before leaving for the evening, and was usually able to do so. His staff summed up their feelings by saying that they felt they were working with him rather than for him.

The new government faced little sustained opposition in the first session of the new Parliament and had no difficulty getting its legislation approved. One of the first important measures introduced was a bill to provide financial assistance to the provincial governments for a transcontinental highway. It is hard for us to realize that in 1949 it was not possible to drive across Canada from one end to the other without making diversions into the United States from both Ontario and British Columbia. In Newfoundland there was no road of any kind for more than half the distance across the province. The reason there was no highway across Canada was that roads were a provincial responsibility, and several of the provincial governments did not place high priority on building roads through sparsely populated areas. The construction of a trans-Canadian highway had been enthusiastically supported by the National Liberal Convention of 1948. St. Laurent felt bound to proceed with this national project though he knew that the Quebec government under Maurice Duplessis would not participate. There was, in fact, a road across Quebec, but it was far below Trans-Canada standards. It was not until eleven years later, under a new provincial government, that Quebec agreed to accept federal assistance for the Trans-Canada Highway.

St. Laurent attached even greater importance to removing the two

ANNO TRICESIMO

VICTORIÆ REGINÆ.

****

C A P. III.

An Act for the Union of *Canada, Nova Scotia*, and *New Brunswick*, and the Government thereof; and for Purposes connected therewith. *[29th March 1867.]*

WHEREAS the Provinces of *Canada, Nova Scotia*, and *New Brunswick* have expressed their Desire to be federally united into One Dominion under the Crown of the United Kingdom of *Great Britain* and *Ireland*, with a Constitution similar in Principle to that of the United Kingdom :

And whereas such a Union would conduce to the Welfare of the Provinces and promote the Interests of the *British* Empire :

And whereas on the Establishment of the Union by Authority of Parliament it is expedient, not only that the Constitution of the Legislative Authority in the Dominion be provided for, but also that the Nature of the Executive Government therein be declared :

And whereas it is expedient that Provision be made for the eventual Admission into the Union of other Parts of *British North America* :

Be it therefore enacted and declared by the Queen's most Excellent Majesty, by and with the Advice and Consent of the Lords Spiritual

C   and

Under the terms of the BNA Act of 1867, Canada's constitution could only be changed by the British Parliament.

last remnants of Canada's former colonial status. In 1949 the Supreme Court of Canada was not the final court of appeal for Canadian lawsuits; appeals could still be taken to the Judicial Committee of the British Privy Council, which had been the Supreme Court of the British Empire. St. Laurent endeavoured to have the Supreme Court of Canada made supreme in fact as well as in name. The legislation passed easily in the new Parliament.

He also hoped to end the necessity of going to the British Parliament for amendments to the Canadian Constitution. In order to make this happen, it was necessary to find an "amending formula" which would permit Canada to alter its own Constitution in a way

St. Laurent pursued less stressful endeavours when not in office

that would be acceptable to both federal and provincial governments. Here St. Laurent was not so successful. It was relatively easy to get the British Parliament to amend the BNA Act so Canada could amend its own Constitution in purely federal matters. The difficulty lay in the division of power between federal and provincial governments. By September, 1950, in spite of lengthy negotiations, no progress had been made. St. Laurent decided to give up hope of "patriating" the Constitution.

Chapter 4
Prime Minister at Large

The first year following the 1949 election was easier than any other for Prime Minister St. Laurent. During 1950, however, his leadership was tested by a succession of crises.

First, a flood in Manitoba's Red River Valley reached the proportions of a national disaster. Although the federal government eventually dealt generously with the problems of relief and rehabilitation, St. Laurent's initial reaction was not too sympathetic, and he began to lose support in the West. Then, in the late summer of 1950, all railway operations in Canada were halted when railworkers went on strike for better pay. St. Laurent had personally intervened to try and prevent the strike; now, he summoned a special session of Parliament which passed unprecedented legislation ordering the strikers to return to work. In spite of his smooth handling of the debate in Parliament, it was an anxious time for St. Laurent.

Meanwhile, an even graver crisis was brewing. At the end of June, 1950, Communist North Korea attacked South Korea. President Truman at once declared American support for South Korea, and provided military aid. The United Nations Security Council endorsed the American action and urged member countries to assist in restoring peace.

As a member of the United Nations, Canada was called upon to make a contribution. St. Laurent, who was deeply committed to the principles of international co-operation which the UN represented, did not hesitate. Parliament approved his proposed measures for involvement with the UN in Korea and with NATO in Europe, and for increased defence expenditure. Once again, the possibility of sending Canadian armed forces overseas raised the spectre of another conscription crisis. George Drew and the Toronto *Globe and Mail* tried to inflame the issue, but there was barely a word of protest from French Canada over the question of sending troops abroad. St. Laurent was trusted when he declared simply that conscription would not be necessary.

In 1951, in view of the increase in defence expenditures, Parliament was asked to grant the government emergency powers to regulate the economy and establish a department of defence production.

These measures were passed without difficulty, but their existence was to create problems for the government after the fighting ended in Korea.

By 1950, there had been a virtual revolution in the conduct of Canada's external and defence policies. After the war, Mackenzie King had yearned to return to the semi-isolationism which characterized the period between the wars. In contrast, St. Laurent felt Canada should have an active role in international affairs, and a full share of responsibility for the maintenance of peace and security in the world. This change of direction was not the work of St. Laurent alone. With Pearson responsible for external affairs, Brooke Claxton for defence and C.D. Howe for defence production, St. Laurent had an exceptionally able team. But St. Laurent was the undoubted captain, and his interest was not limited to external relationships: he was at least equally interested in domestic policies. He was generally as familiar with the subject under cabinet consideration as the minister presenting it. St. Laurent's policy in government was to maintain a coherent pattern of decisions and actions, based upon practicality and sound financial management.

In 1949, soon after becoming prime minister, St. Laurent announced that one of his government's urgent concerns was to improve the lot of senior citizens by making old age pensions more widely available. The revision of the old age security law was to be one of the major achievements of his years in office.

Lester B. Pearson, who later became prime minister, was a close colleague of St. Laurent, and one of Canada's most respected external affairs ministers. He was awarded the 1957 Nobel Peace Prize for resolving the Suez crisis of 1956.

From its beginning in 1927, old age pensioning had been administered by provincial governments, though some funds came from the federal treasury. Pensions were paid to needy persons over seventy years of age. An applicant's need was determined by a severe provincial means test, during which the individual was required to state how much savings and property they held. This means test was felt by many to be a degrading invasion of privacy, with the result that many people who were in need of assistance refused to apply for it. St. Laurent's objective was to provide everybody over seventy with an old age pension *without* the need of a means test. The new "universal" pensions, which were to be based on contributions made during the working life of Canadians, were to be federally administered. To accomplish this, an amendment of the Constitution at a federal-provincial conference in December, 1950, would be required.

St. Laurent managed the conference very cleverly. He first had the ministers of external affairs and defence present the sombre realities of world affairs, including the fighting in Korea and the military build-up within the Atlantic Alliance to counter the Soviets. Next, the minister of finance pointed out the limitation which defence costs placed on federal expenditures in other fields.

St. Laurent then announced that the federal government was prepared to renew existing tax agreements with the provinces. Against such a gloomy background, this seemed to be a generous offer. At the same time, he asked the provincial premiers to approve the plan to establish a national system of contributory old age pensions. It was known that nine provincial premiers would support such an amendment. The surprise was the attitude of Premier Duplessis, who indicated that Quebec might also agree.

While St. Laurent was a minister and then a new prime minister, Duplessis treated him with what some might call contempt, for Duplessis thought St. Laurent was politically naive. St. Laurent's victory in the 1949 election had established his credentials as a professional politician. His courtesy and persuasiveness in 1950 drew further admiration from Duplessis, who said, "You did not try to force your opinion on anyone; you left the door open for friendly discussion, and I think that is the basis upon which it is possible to arrive at definite and just results that we all hope will be achieved. For your courtesy we congratulate and thank you."

St. Laurent personally drafted the constitutional amendment to which the provincial governments agreed, and it was enacted by British Parliament. The old age security legislation was endorsed by Canadian Parliament in 1951 and the universal pension paid from January 1, 1952. No one doubted that St. Laurent alone won Duplessis's agreement.

Unfortunately, such co-operation between the federal government and the govern-

St. Laurent travelled from coast to coast on election campaigns and won support among all Canadians. He is pictured here talking to a fisherman in the Maritimes.

ment of Quebec was unusual. Often, not even St. Laurent's powers of conciliation or his natural sympathy with French Canada could bridge the gap between Quebec City and Ottawa.

In the years after World War II, Canadian universities were sustained by federal grants to war veterans who wanted to continue their education. By 1951, the veterans' education programme was complete. The universities were soon in urgent need of financial assistance. The Royal Commission on the Arts, Letters and Sciences, presided over by Vincent Massey, recommended the provision of direct federal grants to support Canadian universities. The grants were to be awarded automatically; that is, there was to be no arbitrary discrimination between universities. Nevertheless, St. Laurent feared that the grants would be regarded by Duplessis as an intrusion into the provinces' exclusive control over education. His fears proved well-founded. When the grant proposal was first voted on in 1951, it was strongly attacked by Quebec nationalists, though it was accepted in the other nine provinces. Duplessis would agree only to a compromise in which cheques were signed by the finance ministers of Quebec and of Canada. The next year he abandoned the compromise and forbade universities in Quebec to accept federal grants, which he said were a menace to Quebec's autonomy. In spite of the fact that the prime minister of Canada was French Canadian, mistrust of Ottawa still ran deep in many parts of Quebec.

During his years in office, St. Laurent consistently supported Canadian involvement in international affairs. He encouraged official visits to Ottawa by representatives of foreign governments and, from the beginning of 1951, became increasingly involved in travel outside Canada. At a meeting of Commonwealth prime ministers in London in 1951, St. Laurent struck up a friendship with Indian prime minister, Jawaharlal Nehru. In Paris, St. Laurent was cordially received by the president and prime minister. He was also acclaimed by the French press. The presence of the French-speaking prime minister of Canada, with his dignity and charm, seemed to be a tonic for a country just beginning to recover from the war and occupation. He was deeply affected by his reception in the land of his forbears.

In 1951, St. Laurent was called upon to welcome Princess Elizabeth and her husband Prince Philip when they visited Canada. The prime minister had had misgivings about the visit, and tried to discourage it. The king was seriously ill. Supposing he died while his heir was in Canada? Happily he did not, and the royal visit proved enormously popular.

Louis St. Laurent was almost fanatically punctual. He did not like to be kept waiting, and he hated to be late. His staff had no success in persuading him that he should never arrive early at receptions at which

The royal visit of Princess Elizabeth and Prince Philip in 1951 was a great success

he was to be principal guest. In vain, they pointed out that the formal arrangements for receiving him were often not completed until the last moment before his expected arrival. If the distinguished guest arrived before the preparations were complete, it could (and often did) cause great embarrassment.

In 1951, for instance, Princess Elizabeth and Prince Philip often moved from place to place too fast. On the day they visited the Houses of Parliament, they were to be received at the main door by the prime minister and Mrs. St. Laurent. The royal couple was ahead of schedule and St. Laurent was not at the door in time to greet the visitors. The prime minister made no comment on this incident, but he was aware of the irony and amusement it created among his staff. His lesson well learned, St. Laurent never again arrived early at a reception given in his honour. In his travels around the country, he was often to be seen pacing up and down his private railway car for a full five minutes before the appointed time of a visit, looking impatiently at his watch but never emerging until the exact moment had come.

One of the most distasteful questions St. Laurent had to deal with during 1950 and 1951 was how to safeguard the country against subversive activities. At that time, relations between the United States and the Soviet Union were particularly tense. During this Cold War, a group of Americans led by Senator Joseph McCarthy waged a campaign of terror against alleged Communists. This anti-communist feeling spilled over into Canada, and rumours of a communist infiltration of the civil service began to circulate. Remembering the evidence uncovered during the Gouzenko affair, Canadians seemed ready to believe the rumours. Suspicions of communist infiltration threatened to become as inflated an issue in Canada as it was in the United States.

St. Laurent took a firm stand. In Parliament he explained the basis on which security screening – the investigation of a suspected individual's background – was done. He stressed the importance of secrecy in screening if the reputations of innocent people were to be protected. He was determined to avoid public inquiries, fearing that they would become witch hunts and spectator sports. Often, as the example in the United States illustrated, the stigma of an investigation into communist activities was difficult for anyone to shake, even if the investigation itself revealed no grounds for suspicion.

Speaking with conviction and sincerity, St. Laurent argued that the best method for combating communism at home was to make democracy work for the whole population. The freedom of expression which Canada allowed communist organizations was itself an illustration of the contrast between free and totalitarian countries. In an emphatic conclusion, the prime minister observed that he would be sorry to see it become a crime in Canada merely to hold opinions. St. Laurent's liberal attitude helped defuse a potential crisis which threatened to erupt on more than one occasion.

In late 1950, the cost of living in Canada began to rise and continued to do so throughout 1951. The CCF pressed the government to use its emergency powers legislation to control prices. St. Laurent knew prices had increased because of military expenditures associated with the fighting in Korea and the Cold War. He did not believe price controls in Canada could be used successfully against worldwide inflation and he rejected the demand for them. He felt, however, that some action to bring down prices was needed.

The freedom of Canadian manufacturers to fix the retail price of their products often kept prices higher than they would have been had merchants been free to set their own competitive prices. This price-fixing practice was known as resale price maintenance. The government introduced legislation to prohibit it. A strong lobby developed in the business community against the proposed law and

Louis St. Laurent could not drive. His early attempts to do so caused his family great alarm, and they were relieved when he hired a permanent chauffeur. Here, St. Laurent shows his skills at a more traditional form of transportation.

the Conservatives decided to oppose it strongly.

The debate began on December 17, 1951, and soon developed into a "filibuster." (Filibuster is the name given to the systematic obstruction of a bill's passage through Parliament by stalling procedures such as repeating speeches at every stage of the bill making process.) The filibuster dragged on for several frustrating days. At one point St. Laurent became so exasperated that he threatened to impose closure – that is, to cut off all further debate – but realized in time that this would have given the Opposition new grounds for protest. The bill was finally passed when Parliament was recalled two days after Christmas. This filibuster at the end of 1951 was the first sign that St. Laurent would in future have trouble getting controversial legislation through Parliament.

In January, 1952, St. Laurent was suddenly faced with the duty of recommending a new governor general. He thought he had postponed this task when he persuaded Lord Alexander to extend his term beyond 1951. Then Prime Minister Winston Churchill visited Ottawa and told St. Laurent he would like to have Alexander in the British cabinet as minister of defence. He asked St. Laurent's permission to approach him. St. Laurent agreed; Alexander accepted; and a new governor general had to be chosen without delay. The prime minister felt that national self-esteem required the appointment of a Canadian. His choice was Vincent Massey, who had been Canadian high commissioner in London during the war. King George VI accepted the recommendation with enthusiasm.

St. Laurent was aware that the appointment of a Canadian would be seen by some as a deliberate weakening, by a French Canadian prime minister, of Canada's ties with Britain. To counter this objection, St. Laurent, when asked whether only Canadians would be recommended in future, replied that no such rule was being established, but said he "would not like to admit that Canadians, alone among His Majesty's subjects, should be considered unworthy to represent the King in their own country." Put that way it was hard for any self-respecting Canadian to object, and no one did in public.

Alexander ceased to be governor general on January 28, 1952. A few days later, on February 5, George VI died. St. Laurent felt that the accession of the new Queen should be proclaimed with great solemnity. To witness the historic ceremony he called a meeting of the full Privy Council, including all serving and former cabinet ministers, and a few others especially honoured by appointment.

When, in 1953, the prime minister announced to Parliament the title of the new queen, he made a speech so acceptable to traditionalists that even John Diefenbaker, who spoke for the Conservative Opposition, called it "a most moving address." He also described St. Laurent's speech as evidence that about "the unity that is provided by the Crown, there is no division...but a common devotion."

Vincent Massey, first Canadian governor-general of Canada

Chapter 5
A Tired Leader?

Law student and prime minister: the features changed but the calm, determined expression remained

The most important decision St. Laurent made in 1952 concerned his own future. His position in Parliament was very strong. On December 5, 1951, Liberal MPs held a dinner to celebrate St. Laurent's completion of ten years in public life. Earlier in the day, in the House of Commons, warm tributes were paid to the prime minister by George Drew and spokesmen of the other parties. Drew's former personal hostility to St. Laurent had disappeared. It seemed the prime minister had no enemies in the House. St. Laurent had promised his family he would retire soon after his seventieth birthday, February 1, 1952. He had already carried out his 1949 programme and he thought that at the national convention a new leader would be chosen and new policies established for the party. He wanted to retire well before the next election so the new leader would have a chance to establish himself.

Before he had announced his decision to retire, it began to look as though the government was losing support in the country. In twenty-two by-elections between June, 1949, and the end of 1951, the Conservatives had won only five seats from the Liberals. In May, 1952, there were six by-elections. In three, a Conservative replaced a Liberal; in the other three, Liberal majorities were reduced. Two of the new Conservative members were French-speaking. Liberals felt they were losing ground even in their traditional strongholds. There was growing pressure on St. Laurent to remain leader. In July, 1952, he agreed that, if his retirement might mean the defeat of the government, he would stay on.

Once this decision was made, St. Laurent embarked on a vigorous campaign to revive the party nationwide. In late summer, 1952, he made an extensive tour of the West which really marked the beginning of his second election campaign.

By 1952, the demand for television in Canada was strong. The Massey Commission recommended a television system be started and operated by the Canadian Broadcasting Corporation, which was already responsible for radio broadcasts. St. Laurent was personally unenthusiastic about television, but he realized it could not be delayed much longer. The CBC was authorized to establish television stations in Montreal and Toronto. Broadcasts began in September, 1952. Before long, Ottawa had a television station, and during his western tour, St. Laurent announced that television would soon reach the West, with stations to be established in Vancouver and Winnipeg, as well as in Halifax in the East. In November, 1952, the government authorized the CBC to license private stations. There was to be only one station in each centre, and the private stations were to broadcast CBC programmes. In this way, national coverage would be achieved as quickly as possible. The introduction of television and the abolition of the radio licence fee at the same time were popular political measures which increased public support for the government.

That support was weakened somewhat at the beginning of 1953, when news broke of a scandal in the army. The ministry of defence was

St. Laurent makes a forceful point during a speech

accused of excessive and irrational spending. Orders for thousands of teapots, ties and serving-spoons were itemized in the press, to the amusement of the public. It was reported that army property had been sold by individuals for their own profit. Most embarrassing of all, it was said that horses had been included on the army payroll so pay could be claimed for them. The Opposition protested vociferously about slack administration and abuse. Embarrassed, the Liberals dealt promptly with the charges (most of which had been exaggerated), but although the total sum of money involved in the military scandal was not great, the government's credibility – its very ability to govern – had been called into question. In the short term, the damage did not prove serious, but the incident was a sign that the government was facing more persistent and vigorous opposition.

St. Laurent and most of his senior colleagues attended the coronation of Queen Elizabeth in London on June 2, 1953. Right after the prime minister's return to Ottawa, the cabinet met and decided to call an election for August 10. The campaign of 1953 was a near repetition of the 1949 campaign, and the reception the prime minister received was nearly as enthusiastic. When the results were in, the Liberals had 173 out of 265 seats, as compared with 192 out of 262 in 1949. The main losses were in the West. Only six seats were lost

Brooke Claxton (above), minister of defence and Douglas Abbott, minister of finance, both members of St. Laurent's cabinet

in Ontario and none in Quebec or the Maritimes. Two seats were gained in Newfoundland and the Liberals won the newly created constituency of the Northwest Territories. The 1953 election was a second landslide. Brooke Claxton, the minister who had directed the campaign, wrote: "Once again St. Laurent proved to be the star attraction of the whole campaign. The people love to meet him and hear what he has to say."

The election was followed by three politically quiet months. St. Laurent decided that the time was ripe for him to fulfill a long-standing ambition. It was announced that the prime minister would leave for a world tour on February 4, 1954. In forty-five days St. Laurent visited London, Paris, Bonn and Rome and met with European heads of government. He called at the NATO headquarters in Paris and inspected the Canadian forces in Europe. He made extensive visits to Pakistan and India, and briefer visits to Ceylon

A Tired Leader?

(now Sri Lanka), Indonesia, the Philippines, South Korea, Japan and Hawaii. He inspected the three Canadian destroyers that were in Far Eastern waters and met the Canadian forces still on duty in Korea, where actual fighting had ended months earlier. The strenuous tour was a great success and boosted Canadian prestige in world affairs considerably. Inevitably, though, the tour took its toll on the seventy-two-year-old prime minister. Despite his good health and remarkable ability to overcome fatigue, it took several months for him to recover his customary strength.

Maurice Duplessis, premier of Quebec

Fortunately, the rest of the parliamentary session was not very controversial, and St. Laurent did not have to exert himself unduly. Just after the session ended, St. Laurent lost three senior ministers: Claxton from defence, Abbott from finance, and Chevrier from transport. Their resignations made a reorganization of the cabinet necessary; the government was never as strong again after the loss of these experienced and effective ministers.

St. Laurent's main concern in 1954 was his relationship with the premier of Quebec, Maurice Duplessis. Their personal relations had improved in 1950 and 1951 when Duplessis agreed to the old age pension amendment to the Constitution. Then, early in 1954, the government of Quebec imposed its own personal income tax. This meant residents of Quebec would have to pay two income taxes: one to the provincial government and one to Ottawa.

Back in 1947, tax rental agreements had been made with seven of the nine provincial governments which kept the rate of income tax the same all over Canada, and supplied the poorer provinces with revenue to provide adequate public services. Under the agreements, the federal government imposed the only income tax in the country, and then paid "rental" to the provincial governments. Taxes could thus be collected easily, and the money redistributed fairly. These agreements had been renewed in 1952, when Ontario also made an agreement, but Quebec still refused to participate in the scheme. As a result, though Quebec taxpayers paid federal income tax just as everyone else in Canada, the Quebec government received no rental payment from Ottawa.

Canadians first thought of developing the St. Lawrence river in the nineteenth century, but no realistic plans were drawn up until the 1940s, when the development was proposed as a joint Canadian-American project. The negotiations were beset by problems and dragged on, without American acceptance, until 1951, when Canada announced that it was prepared to go ahead and develop the seaway alone. By this time, thanks to an extensive publicity campaign, Canadians were impatient for construction to begin. The Americans asked for a little more time, and three years later, after more negotiations, an agreement between the two nations was signed and approved by the US Congress. The seaway was one of the major achievements of St. Laurent's government.

Premier Duplessis claimed the provincial tax had priority over the federal tax, and once again accused the central government of trying to undermine provincial autonomy. Many in the federal government felt the people of Quebec should blame their provincial leaders for the double tax burden. But St. Laurent said privately that he did not feel the federal government could continue to treat the people of Quebec unfairly, just because their premier was unreasonable. He felt strongly that some solution must be found. For the first and only time while prime minister, St. Laurent spoke in a budget debate. He offered sincere and genuine readiness "to sit down with the authorities of Quebec" to discuss any alternative to the tax rental agreement, and hoped the government of Quebec would agree to such discussions. Duplessis would not and kept attacking what he called "federal centralization." St. Laurent began to see these attacks as threats to national unity. He decided to attack in his turn. In September, 1954, in a speech to the Quebec Reform Club, St. Laurent asserted that "the province of Quebec can be a province like any other." He spoke spontaneously, with uncharacteristic vehemence. He denied that he was a "centralizer," as Duplessis had charged, and said his intention had certainly not been to erode the autonomy of the provinces. There was, he added, a margin between true provincial autonomy and the kind of autonomy which served as a screen, so that the administration of a province would not be questioned. He declared that, so long as he was prime minister, the

A Tired Leader?

federal government would not accept that any one province was more important than the whole country.

An attack by a prime minister on a provincial premier was unusual in those days. Prime ministers usually endured criticism in silence. The public reaction to St. Laurent's speech was therefore remarkable. In English-speaking Canada, it was widely believed that St. Laurent intended to "put Quebec in its place." Liberals in Quebec expected him to lead a fight to the finish with Duplessis. Few commentators had noted that, in his speech, he had repeated the offer to try to find a mutually satisfactory substitute for the tax rental agreement Duplessis had rejected.

Duplessis, in turn, went on the offensive in a public speech. It seemed a long struggle lay ahead, from which neither the province nor the country could benefit. St. Laurent made no public reply to Duplessis. Shortly afterward, Duplessis telephoned St. Laurent to suggest a meeting in Montreal to seek a solution to the taxation dispute. The meeting was held on October 5 and a compromise was worked out quickly, with both sides making important concessions. The new agreement was offered to all provinces as an alternative to the tax rental agreement: in theory, it was not an exclusive arrangement for Quebec. Quebec was treated as "a province like the others," though no other provincial government accepted the new arrangement. When St. Laurent informed the other premiers of the compromise with Quebec, he said the federal government was not wedded to the principle of tax rental agreements and was ready to consider any better alternative. Any alternative must "make it financially possible for all the provinces, whatever their tax base, to perform their constitutional functions themselves and to provide a reasonable Canadian level of provincial services without an abnormal burden of taxation." This statement was the germ of the system of equalization which was to replace the tax rental system in 1957.

A serious decline in support for the St. Laurent government began in 1955. What weakened the government was a filibuster of a bill to amend the Defence Production Act. The department of defence production had been established in 1951 to deal with Canada's involvement in the Korean War. The department was given many of the arbitrary and drastic powers given to the department of munitions and supply during the Second World War. The department of defence production was intended to be temporary, and the Defence Production Act provided for its abolition in 1956. In 1955, the government decided the department was still necessary, and introduced legislation to remove the expiry date.

In handling this simple measure, the government made almost every mistake imaginable. The bill was introduced by the prime

minister, but management of the debate was left to C.D. Howe, the minister of defence production. The Conservatives concentrated on the arbitrary powers given to the minister, and argued that this was an abuse of Parliamentary power. In the debate, Howe made tactical errors which made it appear he was seeking power for its own sake. The Opposition was supported by most of the press, even strong Liberal newspapers. Sensing that the public was responding favourably to the attack, the Conservative opposition mounted a filibuster. St. Laurent knew the debate was being handled badly, and would have intervened much earlier if a similar situation had arisen in 1952 or 1953. But in the years after 1954, he was subject to occasional periods of depression and apathy, and he sometimes failed to act promptly and decisively in Parliament.

C.D. Howe's handling of the debate on the ministry of defence production and later the pipeline debate brought charges of arrogance and abuse of parliamentary power from the Opposition

Before the debate was over, even Howe realized that some concession was necessary, but the filibuster did not end until he went off on a fishing trip and left management of the debate to St. Laurent and the House leader, Walter Harris. St. Laurent quickly negotiated a compromise with George Drew and the bill passed.

But the damage was already done. The Opposition had successfully portrayed Howe as an arrogant, power-hungry minister who dominated government, and who tried to ride roughshod over the rights of Parliament. St. Laurent was described as an old, tired leader who could no longer control the government. These images persisted after 1955. The Opposition smelled victory. Sensing that the weight of public opinion was shifting in their favour, Conservative MPs lost no opportunity to attack the Liberal government.

Chapter 6
The Pipeline Debate

When Parliament met in January, 1956, neither the government nor the public had any advance warning that a debate over a natural gas pipeline would lead to the most serious upheaval in Parliament since the conscription crisis of 1944.

By 1949, Alberta was producing more natural gas than could be sold in the province, and had begun to look around for export markets. There were two possibilities. The gas producers in Alberta and the province's Social Credit government favoured a policy of exporting Alberta gas to the American midwest, and importing Texan gas to meet the needs of southern Ontario. It was a continental approach; that is, it viewed the question from a North American, rather than a specifically Canadian, perspective.

C.D. Howe, on the other hand, though he had been born in the United States, was committed to strengthening Canada's industrial base. He felt that an assured supply of Canadian energy was essential to national development. He favoured a pipeline that would run west-east through Canadian territory, supplying Albertan gas to consumers across Canada. He was

Jeanne and Louis St. Laurent in Ottawa

inflexible in his opposition to the continental approach, and St. Laurent supported him strongly.

In 1951, Parliament incorporated a company called TransCanada PipeLines. The company's Texan backers undertook the building of an all-Canadian pipeline from Alberta to Montreal. In 1953, the federal government announced that natural gas could only be exported from Canada if there was no use for it within Canada: Canadian needs would have to be satisfied first. The government would permit the export of only *surplus* gas to the American midwest, through Manitoba.

Throughout 1954, TransCanada PipeLines tried to raise the capital needed to build the pipeline. The company was unsuccessful, and it became clear that the project would founder without financial support from the government. TransCanada began discussions with Ottawa in January, 1955, but most of that year was lost because the company and the government were unable to reach an agreement. Late in 1955, TransCanada stated its position: the company could raise the capital to build the line across the prairies, but needed help to build the section from the Manitoba-Ontario border to Kapuskasing. The governments of Canada and Ontario would establish a joint crown company to build that section as a government project and then lease or sell it to TransCanada. Ontario PipeLine Crown Corporation passed the Ontario legislature easily. There seemed little reason to anticipate any serious difficulty in Parliament in 1956. It was expected the CCF would advocate government ownership of the whole line, but there was no reason to expect the Conservative Opposition to oppose a project so strongly supported by the Conservative government of Ontario. Before Parliament had time to deal with the bill to establish the crown corporation, TransCanada was forced to admit it would need help to finance the rest of the pipeline. In early May, the government finally agreed on a short-term loan to TransCanada. The loan included a condition that, if the company defaulted, all its assets would become the property of the crown. In that case the pipeline could be completed as a government project.

The pipeline project was much greater in magnitude, cost and complexity than the St. Lawrence Seaway had been. Its construction should have been a source of national pride. Looking back, it seems the government's first mistake was not undertaking a publicity campaign similar to the campaign for the St. Lawrence Seaway. A campaign stressing the value to Manitoba, Northern Ontario and Central Canada of a supply of Canadian gas might have captured the public imagination. Instead, the government said almost nothing and the pipeline was portrayed by the Opposition as a sell-out to Texan millionaires by the arrogant, American-born C.D. Howe. The battle for public support was lost before the debate began.

The debate in Parliament might have been easier to manage if the introduction of the legislation had not been delayed until early May. Parliamentary approval was required by June 7, 1956, if construction was to start that year. There was less than a month to get the bill passed. Failure to start the pipeline in 1956 would have made it almost impossible for the company to keep its private financial backing for another year. In that case, the pipeline would have been delayed indefinitely and, perhaps, never built.

Even before the pipeline legislation was introduced in Parliament, both Conservatives and the CCF had undertaken to obstruct it systematically. In doing so, they had the support of almost all parliamentary reporters from the press, radio and the new medium of television. Hardly a voice was raised in the media in favour of the all-Canadian pipeline. The House leader, Walter Harris, realized that the pipeline legislation could not be passed by the deadline without the use of the closure rule, which cut short debate and thus saved time. Closure had last been used in 1932, and hardly anyone in Parliament was familiar with it. Closure had always been opposed by the Liberal party as a restriction on freedom of debate in Parliament, and its use was likely to create a bigger political issue than the pipeline itself. The government had to decide whether the pipeline was worth the political risk. The cabinet was divided, so the final decision was made by St. Laurent himself. He decided that closure should be imposed. Even with closure, he reasoned, there were still three full weeks for debate.

Very few members of the cabinet except St. Laurent and Harris realized how complicated the use of closure would be. The pipeline measure was a money bill. Under the antiquated rules of the House used in 1956, there were four separate votes on a money bill. Howe, who did not understand the procedural complications, left the management of the debate almost entirely to Harris. After the Opposition had stalled the debate for two days by raising all sorts of procedural objections, Harris decided that closure, which itself required two days each time it was used, would have to be applied at all four stages of the proceedings.

St. Laurent was criticized for his apparent apathy during the debate's early stages. He did not make his first speech until May 22, two weeks after the pipeline measure was introduced. He then made a brief presentation of the case for the pipeline and expressed his regret that closure had to be imposed. He said the government believed it was in the interests of the Canadian people to get the pipeline started at once; he asserted that the majority in the House had a right to have a decision made while that decision could still be effective. Notwithstanding St. Laurent's appeal, stalling continued. In the committee

Two Conservative leaders, John Diefenbaker (standing) and George Drew

stage of the bill, the opportunities for obstruction were almost unlimited. The proceedings were very disorderly on May 24 and 25. Following an appeal from St. Laurent on May 28, the House grew calmer, and for the next three days the pipeline was actually debated.

A series of diversionary tactics on May 31 almost scuttled the bill. It was saved on June 1 by the Speaker's extraordinary proposal that the House "blot out" all the proceedings of the previous day after 5:00 p.m. This was unprecedented, and pandemonium broke out when the Speaker made his proposal. The Opposition refused to vote on it, but it was adopted anyway. That night, closure was imposed and the pipeline bill passed the committee stage. The Opposition and the press, charging the government with arrogant abuse of parliamentary procedure, termed June 1, 1956, "Black Friday."

After further last-ditch attempts to thwart its progress, the pipeline bill passed its third reading on June 5, two days before the

The final weld which completed the TransCanada PipeLines natural gas line from Alberta to Montreal, Oct. 10, 1958, at Kapuskasing, Ont.

deadline. After a speedy passage through the Senate, the bill received Royal Assent on June 6, the day construction was to start.

St. Laurent's government had ensured that the longest pipeline in the world would be built in Canada but the future of the government itself was by no means secure. Its image had been badly damaged by the acrimonious pipeline debate, and the Opposition had grown stronger.

St. Laurent suspected that the Opposition might take the opportunity of trying to force an election by withholding "supply." Supply is the name given to the money which Parliament uses to pay the costs of government. Supply is voted, or approved by Parliament, for a year at a time and the voting of supply is the ultimate control the House of Commons has over the cabinet. The fiscal year begins on April 1, but the whole of supply is never voted until all the government's expenditure estimates have been approved. Meanwhile, something called "interim supply" is voted in grants for a month or so at a time.

By June 7, 1956, Parliament had not yet voted any interim supply to allow the government to carry on beyond May 31. If a grant was not approved before June 15, the government would not be able to pay its bills, including the salaries of public servants.

When the government asked for interim supply on June 11, St. Laurent and most of the ministers believed it would not be granted in time. The Opposition could easily prolong the debate for several weeks, knowing that the government would not dare use the closure rule again. If supply was not available in time, the government would have no choice but to dissolve Parliament and call a general election, which the Liberals would probably lose. Grimly, St. Laurent and his ministers took their places in Parliament on the afternoon of the supply debate. They were astounded when George Drew rose and announced that supply would not be opposed by the Conservatives. For the time being, the government was saved.

The St. Lawrence Seaway was one of the major achievements of St. Laurent's government

The Pipeline Debate

Chapter 7
The Last Election

St. Laurent acknowledges the cheers of supporters

The later stages of the pipeline debate had seemed to galvanize St. Laurent into a new period of activity. The following nine months were a source of achievement for his government. Instead of ending the session of Parliament as soon as possible, the government introduced legislation to establish a new plan of tax sharing and equalization which replaced tax rental agreements in 1957. From the time the compromise was made with Duplessis in 1954, St. Laurent had been determined to find a substitute for the tax rental system which would be acceptable to the government of Quebec while meeting the financial needs of the other provinces. He had been very active at federal-provincial conferences in 1955 and 1956, while working out the new plan. The plan was outlined in the federal budget in March, 1956, and no objection was made to the principle of equalization by any provincial government, though all would have liked to get a larger share of the tax revenues. For St. Laurent, the great advantage was that equalization would meet both the fiscal needs of the poorer provinces and acceptance by Duplessis. The bill passed smoothly through Parliament.

The autumn of 1956 was a quiet period even after St. Laurent had announced in September that he expected to lead the government in one more election. Part of the reason for the tranquility was Drew's retirement due to ill health. Until the Conservatives could hold a convention and choose a new leader, Earl Rowe served as acting leader. He had no incentive to stir up controversy. St. Laurent was solicitous about Drew's future and offered him a senatorship, an unusual gesture which was appreciated by Drew's friends.

The one serious controversy the government faced between the pipeline debate and the election of 1957 was over the Israeli, French and British attack on the Suez Canal. When the government of Egypt nationalized the canal in July, 1956, Britain and France were outraged. They tried to organize an international protest. The United States refused to join in the protest and the St. Laurent government tried not to become involved. The Conservative Opposition, however, speaking through John Diefenbaker, urged support for "the United Kingdom in this hour of great stress and difficulty."

Israel had been denied use of the canal by the Egyptian owners. When the canal was attacked on October 29, 1956, Israel was in the forefront, closely supported by Britain and France. St. Laurent regarded the attack on Egypt as an act of aggression contrary to the Charter of the United Nations, as did President Eisenhower, but the positions taken by the United States and Canada were quite different. Eisenhower was ready to have the United States join the Soviet Union in condemning Britain and France as aggressors. St. Laurent and Pearson were anxious to avoid criticizing these two nations which had major historic connections with Canada. They worked actively for a compromise which would end the fighting and restore the unity of the free world. With the full backing of St. Laurent, Pearson succeeded in securing the support of all the free nations for the establishment of the United Nations Emergency Force.

The Conservative charge that St. Laurent was anti-British might have fizzled out if Parliament did not have to meet to approve the expenditures for Canada's share in the Emergency Force. In the debate, Earl Rowe, the acting leader of the Opposition, attacked the government for failing to support Britain. The charge angered St. Laurent. He had been disillusioned at the way powerful nations such as Britain, France, the United States and the Soviet Union had been willing to exploit the United Nations for their own ends. When it served their purposes, they upheld its charter; when it did not, they used their powers of veto to render the UN ineffectual. St. Laurent always sympathized with the problems of the less powerful. One of the purposes of the United Nations, which St. Laurent had always supported, had been to protect weak nations from exploitation by the strong. Now, St. Laurent saw the manipulation of power within the UN itself. He had been "scandalized" by the abuse of the veto by larger powers, who were obviously unwilling to allow "smaller nations to

On successive election campaigns, St. Laurent won the hearts of Canadians, young and old. A reporter asked him why he spent so much time with the children. "After all," he said, "they can't vote.""No, but their parents can!" replied St. Laurent. Besides, he was able to relax with children, and his natural reserve vanished.

The Last Election

John Diefenbaker becomes leader of the Conservative party, December, 1956.

deal decisively with questions which concerned their vital interests."

"Why should they?" demanded an Opposition member.

Outraged, St. Laurent replied that smaller nations, too, were composed of human beings. "The era when the supermen of Europe could govern the whole world has and is coming pretty close to an end."

His words were seized upon by his opponents. Though he was referring primarily to the end of colonialism in general, his comment was taken to be an attack on Britain and a sneer at Winston Churchill, presumed to be one of the "supermen" in question. Conservatives made the most of the phrase. Those few words – the supermen of Europe – probably cost the Liberal government more seats in the 1957 election than anything else St. Laurent said or did in his whole political career.

John Diefenbaker became leader of the Conservative party, and leader of the Opposition, in December, 1956. St. Laurent faced him across the House when Parliament met in January, 1957. Diefenbaker spent relatively little time in Parliament, feeling it was more useful to conduct a pre-election campaign across the country.

The session of 1957 went well for the prime minister, who seemed to have recovered his former vitality. The day the session opened, he intervened personally to settle a nationwide strike on the Canadian Pacific Railway. In Parliament, St. Laurent put through legislation to establish the Canada Council. On his initiative, the government doubled annual grants to universities and created a capital fund to assist in providing buildings and other facilities for the arts and humanities. With St. Laurent's active support, Paul Martin, as minister of health, piloted a bill through Parliament which would eventually provide federal financial assistance for hospital insurance. St. Laurent also took an active part in deciding on priorities for the budget of 1957. Several measures of special benefit to the depressed Maritime provinces were included, family allowances were increased and old age pensions were raised slightly.

On St. Laurent's seventy-fifth birthday, February 1, 1957, the Liberal party held a huge dinner in Quebec City to demonstrate party solidarity. No one asked whether advertising the age of an elderly prime minister was a good opening for an election campaign.

Nevertheless, in April it was announced that a general election would be held on June 10. When the campaign began, it was generally expected that St. Laurent's government would win a third election, but with a reduced majority – this was the opinion of the press and most observers throughout the campaign, despite the realization that St. Laurent's campaign efforts were dismal. In the 1957 election campaign, television was used for the first time. St. Laurent did not like television and refused to adapt himself to the new medium. His first broadcast was delivered in a dull, wooden fashion; the leader had no election theme; the government's past record lacked appeal in 1957; the pipeline debate and charges that the government had ridden roughshod over the rights of Parliament, its attitude during the Suez crisis, the phrase "the supermen of Europe" and the only slight increase in old age pensions all had negative effects. Yet almost no one predicted a Liberal defeat.

The shock was therefore great when the people elected seven more Conservative members than Liberals. It was not a crushing defeat, particularly since the Liberals had received nearly a quarter of a million more votes than the Conservatives. The twenty-five CCF MPs and the nineteen Social Creditors could have tipped the scale either way in Parliament. But St. Laurent was not even slightly interested in meeting Parliament to seek a vote of confidence as Mackenzie King had done after the 1925 election. The Liberals had emerged without elected ministers in five of the ten provinces. In Ontario, only two ministers survived. The defeat of Howe and Harris was a severe blow. St. Laurent regarded the outcome as a moral defeat and resigned as soon as Diefenbaker was ready to form a government. He ceased to

Fishing was one of St. Laurent's favourite recreations

The Last Election

be prime minister on June 21, 1957.

St. Laurent accepted defeat calmly. He arranged for the change of government without apparent emotion, and seemed ready and willing to carry on for some time as the leader of the Opposition in the new Parliament. He went to his summer home on the lower St. Lawrence to rest for a month or two before Parliament reconvened. As soon as he was away from Ottawa, it became obvious that he had been deeply wounded by his first failure in seventy-five years. He sank into a profound depression from which almost nothing could stir him. Alarmed, his wife and children insisted he seek medical advice. The advice came and he announced early in September that he would retire from the leadership of the Liberal party as soon as a new leader could be chosen. A convention was set for early January, 1958.

Meanwhile, St. Laurent recovered sufficiently to carry on as leader of the Opposition when Parliament met in October. He did not choose an interim leader since he felt such a choice might influence the convention. As soon as Lester B. Pearson was chosen leader of the Liberal party, St. Laurent ceased to serve as leader of the Opposition. He was not even in Ottawa when Parliament was

Pierre Trudeau, shown here attending Lester Pearson's funeral in 1972, was St. Laurent's surprise choice for future Liberal leadership

dissolved on February 1, 1958. He took no part in the ensuing election and never again participated actively in public life, though he made occasional appearances at national Liberal party conferences.

During 1958, his health improved and he was able to resume the practice of law in Quebec City, though he never again went into the law courts. The retirement years from 1959 to 1966 revived his good spirits. He and his wife lived a quiet life surrounded by their children and grandchildren. Then, in November, 1966, Jeanne St. Laurent died. Life for St. Laurent was never the same again. Theirs had been an exceptionally happy marriage and he had depended greatly on his wife for companionship and encouragement.

Yet his health remained sound throughout 1967. He was in good spirits when he met his many former colleagues and associates after the state funeral for Vincent Massey in Ottawa in 1967. In the same year, Pearson had just announced he intended to retire and there was keen interest in the succession. St. Laurent surprised one or two former colleagues by voicing the opinion privately that Pierre Trudeau should be the next Liberal leader. At that time, Trudeau's name had not been mentioned seriously by anyone.

Early in 1968, St. Laurent broke his hip and was disabled for the rest of his life. The years until his death in 1973 were increasingly sad, despite the devotion of his family and friends. St. Laurent remained alert to the end, though he was often irritated by his failure to remember names. He died peacefully on July 25, 1973. After a state funeral in Quebec City, his body was taken in a funeral procession to his birthplace, Compton, for burial. The national tributes were impressive but nothing was more moving than the people who gathered in the villages and towns of rural Quebec to watch the procession pass by.

It became the fashion in his lifetime, and even more after his death, to describe Louis St. Laurent as a great gentleman. The description is apt, for St. Laurent's words and actions were always characterized by courtesy and fair-mindedness. But in describing St. Laurent as a gentleman, there is often the implication that "Uncle Louis" was a genial old man who was prime minister in a quiet period when decisive leadership was not required. That patronizing assessment overlooks his many great achievements.

St. Laurent negotiated the union of Newfoundland with Canada which completed Confederation, and his government initiated three great national construction projects: the Trans-Canada Highway, the St. Lawrence Seaway and the natural gas pipeline from Alberta to Montreal. Under his leadership, the Supreme Court of Canada became truly supreme when appeals to the British Privy Council were abolished, and the Canadian Parliament won the power to amend its own Constitution in exclusively federal matters.

St. Laurent recommended the appointment of the first Canadian governor general, and appointed the Royal Commission on Arts, Letters and Sciences which recommended federal grants to the universities, nationwide television and the establishment of the Canada Council; all these recommendations were adopted by the government.

In the field of social security, St. Laurent's government provided universal pensions without a means test for persons over seventy; extended unemployment insurance to cover seasonal workers and fishermen; made legal provision for future federal financial support for hospital insurance; and negotiated the plan of equalization of provincial revenues which contributes so greatly to national unity.

In world affairs, St. Laurent's greatest achievement was to promote active Canadian participation. He was a committed supporter of the North Atlantic Alliance and the United Nations, and his government stationed Canadian troops in Europe and Korea without causing undue protest in Canada. The United Nations Emergency Force which restored peace in Suez was deployed at Canada's suggestion.

These were the achievements of a government which balanced the budget almost every year and reduced the national debt substantially. Despite this record, St. Laurent's years as prime minister continue to be described as quiet, when leadership was not tested by any major crisis. The reason probably is that St. Laurent had an uncanny way of making government seem effortless. He gave the impression that Canada was an easy country to govern. That was not its reputation before 1948, and St. Laurent had not been out of office for two years before Canada once more began to appear a very difficult country to govern.

Louis St. Laurent had many advantages. He was a French Canadian who belonged to both historic cultures and spoke both official languages fluently. He had as fine an intelligence as was ever applied to the problems of government in Canada, a high sense of duty, a capacity to learn and to understand, a breadth of sympathy and a wide knowledge of the country. He represented in his own person the things that unite Canadians.

Yet in 1947, at age seventy-five, his powers had begun to decline. It was fortunate for his reputation that he could leave office with honour and the abiding respect of supporters and opponents alike. His years in public life represented a great career begun when most people are thinking of retirement. He left Canada a richer, a more generous and a more united country than it had been before he became prime minister.

The Last Election

Louis Stephen St. Laurent

1882	Born in Compton, Quebec
1905	Passes final law exam at l'Université Laval in Quebec City
1908	Marries Jeanne Renault
1914	Becomes a founding member of the Canadian Bar Association
1930	Becomes President of the Canadian Bar Association
1941	Selected Minister of Justice under Mackenzie King
1946	Becomes Minister of External Affairs
1948	Wins Liberal party leadership
1948	Nov. 15 Succeeds Mackenzie King to become Canada's second French Canadian Prime Minister
1949	June 27 Elected Prime Minister with overwhelming majority
1949	Newfoundland enters Confederation
1949	Trans-Canada Highway Act passes initiating construction of the world's longest national highway
1949	Supreme Court of Canada made highest court of appeal in Canada
1952	First universal old age pensions distributed
1952	Vincent Massey appointed first Canadian-born governor general
1954	St. Lawrence Seaway Authority established to construct and operate a Canadian seaway from Montreal to Lake Erie
1956	TransCanada PipeLine Bill approved initiating construction of a 3700 km natural gas pipeline from Burstall, Saskatchewan to Montreal, Quebec
1957	Completes tenure as Prime Minister
1973	July 25 State funeral held for Louis St. Laurent in Quebec City

The Right Honourable Louis Stephen St. Laurent

Further Reading

Bothwell, R. and Kilbourn, *W.C.D. Howe: a biography,* Toronto: McClelland & Stewart, 1979.

Fraser, Blair. *Canada: Postwar to Present,* Toronto: Doubleday, 1967.

Granatstein, J.L. *W.L. Mackenzie King,* Toronto: Fitzhenry & Whiteside Limited, 1976.

Massey, V. *What's past is prologue: the memoirs of Vincent Massey.* Toronto: Macmillan of Canada, 1963.

Pickersgill, J.W. *My Years with Louis St. Laurent; a political memoir.* Toronto: University of Toronto Press, 1975.

Power, C.A. *Party Politician. The Memoirs of Chubby Power,* Toronto: Macmillan of Canada, 1966.

Quinn, Magella. *Louis St. Laurent, 1882-1973* Ottawa: Minister of Supply and Services, 1982

Thomson, Dale C. *Louis St. Laurent: Canadian.* Toronto: Macmillan of Canada, 1967.

Credits

Public Archives of Canada, cover (C-692), title page (PA-123990), and pages 4 (C-18768), 5 (C-9822), 6 (C-10192), 7 (C-9815), (C-9819), 8 (C-9841), 9 (C-9813), (C-9884), 10 (C-61709), (C-10181), 11 (C-18766), 12 (C-9835), 13 (C- 13254), 14 (C-26922), 15 (PA-26987), (C-10185), 16 (C-21529), 18 (PA-107933), 20 (C-23252), 22(PA-123988), 23(PA-123990), 25 (C- 22234), 27 (C-14159), 28 (PA-109485), 31 (PA-123992), 33 (PA-117595), 34(PA-123389), 36 (PA-123994), 38 (C-9879), 39 (C-1015), 40 (C-9829), (C-10461), 41 (C-23255), 42 (PA-52489), (PA-121696), 43 (C-31052), 44 (PA-93725), 46 (C-19380), 47 (C-20620), 50 (C-80883), 51 (C-47009), 52 (PA136706), 53 (C-18732), 55 (PA-123991), 56 (PA-112695), 58 (PA-123993), 59 (PA-121710), 63 (C-692)

Every effort has been made to credit all sources correctly. The author and publisher will welcome information that would allow them to correct any errors or omissions.

Index